WIN

Future-Proofing Your Workforce in the Age of Disengagement

Tracy Levine and Michael Levine,
Michelle Galvani and Jenny O'Donnell,
Chris Butsch

Table of Contents

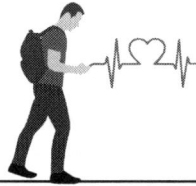

Thank you!

Maximizing shareholder Value can no longer be a company's only purpose!

D ▬▬▬▬
▬▬▬▬▬▬
▬▬▬▬▬▬
▬▬▬▬▬▬
▬▬▬▬▬▬
▬▬▬▬▬▬
▬▬▬▬▬▬
▬▬▬▬▬▬
▬▬▬▬▬▬
▬▬▬▬▬▬

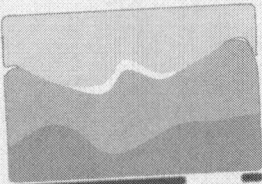

G ▬▬▬▬
▬▬▬▬▬
▬▬▬▬▬
▬▬▬▬▬
▬▬▬▬▬
▬▬▬▬▬
▬▬▬▬▬
▬▬▬▬▬

F ▬▬▬
▬▬▬▬▬
▬▬▬▬▬
▬▬▬▬▬

Statement on the Purpose of a Corporation

"We share a fundamental commitment to all of our stakeholders... we commit to investing in our employees."

Business Roundtable, Statement on the Purpose of a Corporation, August 2019

Companies signing:

A: A.O. Smith Corporation, Abbott, Accenture, ADP, AECOM, The AES Corporation, Aflac, AK Steel Holding Corporation, Allergan, Alliant Energy, Altec Inc., Amazon, American Airlines, American Electric Power, American Express, American Tower Corporation, Ameriprise Financial, Anthem, Inc., AON, Apple, Aramark, Assurant, AT&T Inc. **B:** Ball Corporation, Bank of America, Baxter International Inc., Bayer USA, BCG, Bechtel Corporation, Best Buy Co, Inc Blackrock, BNY Mellon, Boeing, BorgWarner, BP plc, Bristol-Myers Squibb Company **C:** C.V. Starr & Co, Inc., The Carlyle Group, Caterpillar Inc., CBRE Group, Inc., CF Industries Holdings, Inc., Chevron Corporation, Chubb Limited, Cigna, Cisco Systems, Inc., Citi, CNH Industrial, The Coca-Cola Company, Cognizant, Comcast Corporation, ConocoPhillips, Corning Incorporated, Cummins, CVS Health **D:** Day& Zimmermann Inc, Dell, Deloitte, Dow, Duke Energy Corporation, DXC Technology

WIN

E: Eastman Chemical Company, Eaton Corporation Inc, Edison International, ExxonMobil, EY **F:** FedEx Corporation, FIS, Flex Ltd., Fluor Corporation, Ford Motor Company, Fox Corporation, Freeport-McMoRan Inc. **G:** General Dynamics Corporation, General Motors, The Goldman Sachs Group, Inc., The Guardian Life Insurance Company of America **H:** Hanesbrands Inc, Harman International Industries, Inc., Hearst, The Home Depot, Inc., Honeywell International, Inc., Huntington Ingalls Industries **I:** IBM, Infor, The International Paper Company, The Interpublic Group of Companies, ITC Holdings Corp **J:** Jacobs, John Deere, Johnson & Johnson, Johnson Controls International plc, JPMorgan Chase & Co **K:** KeyCorp, Kiewit Corporation, KPMG **L:** L3Harris Technologies, Land O'Lakes, Inc., Leidos, Lennar Corporation, Lockheed Martin Corporation, LyondellBasell Industries **M:** Macy's, Mallinckrodt Pharmaceuticals, Marathon Oil, Marathon Petroleum, Marriott International, MassMutual, Mastercard, McCormick and Company, McKesson Corporation, Medtronic plc, Metlife, Inc., Micron Technology, Inc., Moelis & Company, Morgan Stanley, Motorola Solutions, Inc. **N:** The NASDAQ Composite, National Gypsum Company, The New York Life Insurance Company, Noble Energy, Inc., Northro p Grumman Corporation, Novelis Inc., NRG Energy, Inc. **O:** Oracle Corporation, Owens Corning **P:** PepsiCo, Pfizer Inc., Phillips, Pitney Bowes, Principal, Procter & Gamble, Progressive, PricewaterhouseCoopers **Q:** Qualcomm Incorporated, Quanta **R:** Raytheon,Rockwell Automation, Inc. **S:** S&P Global Inc., Salesforce.com, Inc., SAP, SAS Institute, Schnitzer Steel Industries, Inc., Sempra Energy, Siemens Corporation USA, Silver Lake, Southern Company, Stanley Black & Decker, Inc., Steelcase, Stryker Corporation, Suffolk Construction Company

PROLOGUE

T: Target Corporation, TC Energy, Telephone & Data Systems, Inc., Texas Instruments Incorporated, Tishman Speyer Properties, The Travelers Companies, Inc., TSYS, Turner Construction Company **U:** Union Pacific, United Airlines, Inc., United Technologies Corporation, UPS, USAA **V:** The Vanguard Group, Verisk Analytics, Inc., Visa Inc., Vista Equity Partners, Vistra Energy, Walgreens Boots Alliance, Inc., **W:** Walmart Inc., WESCO International, Inc., Western & Southern Financial Group, The Western Union Company, The Whirlpool Corporation, WIPRO Group, World Fuel Services Corporation, World Wide Technology, Inc., **X:** Xerox Holdings Corporation, Xylem Inc, **Z:** Zebra Technologies Corporation, The 3M Company

3

Chapter 1

Welcome to WIN

The Future of Employee Engagement is Complex

Tracy Levine, Michael Levine,
Michelle Galvani, Jenny O'Donnell,
Chris Butsch

Ask executives about the state of the job market and the workplace; you will get a variety of answers. There is a mixture of excitement and fear as these executives are faced with the complex task of, 'How to Navigate a Future No One can Predict.'

The majority agree that the uncertainty of what the workplace will look like in the future has eroded the trust that once existed between employers and employees.

The current employer and employee relationship is a minefield of distrust and finger pointing. Employees want their employers to provide a clear pathway for career success in exchange for loyalty. In the race for top talent, Corporate leaders promise traditional pathways for career success that may no longer work, and they may not be able to deliver on. Broken promises ensue.

The State of Disengagement
In 2015, only 19% of American employees were fully engaged at work.

To address this growing crisis, American companies spend approximately $1 billion each year on engagement solutions, from gamification to feedback platforms.

The result? Full employee engagement declined. By 2018, the percentage of fully engaged employees dropped to 17%.[1]

Improving engagement is the #1 priority for most employers, but existing disconnected solutions are expensive, inadequate, and lead to frustration.

Welcome to Win

As consultants that work with executives to create winning relationship outcomes for both the employer and employee, we know that improving trust and engagement is a complex problem that requires a multi-faceted holistic solution. The five authors of this book are subject-matter experts spanning three generations, we've spent the past several years speaking with thousands of CEOs, VPs of HR, and other C-Suite executives about engagement solutions that STICK.

WIN

What We Learned

Even some of the most proactive executives and employers felt they were still struggling to find the right approach and tools to achieve sustainable, ongoing employee engagement, top talent recruitment, and skills gap management. A few companies are making progress, but in many cases, companies simply don't know where to start.

So, what prevents companies from creating an engagement culture that works? Well, one huge problem is single function tools that address symptoms, not the complex issues that are causing rampant disengagement. The engagement tools do really well addressing pieces of disengagement but don't necessarily work well together because they were not designed to work well together.

What You will Learn

Our goal for this book is to teach you how to apply a more authentic and holistic approach that improves employee engagement. We'll share with you some exciting and surprising new strategies, such as:

• **Admit that corporations have pivoted to a 'just in time' workforce:** Companies want the flexibility to hire specialized skills on-demand, with no long-term commitment. Take steps to upskill your employees to be hired for their next position internally or externally.
• **Workspaces need to be as agile as your workforce:** Just like your employees, your workspace needs to be dynamic and ready for the future. Leveraging your office environment to improve the employee experience is one of the most underutilized advantages in business today.
• **Supporting healthy and impactful employee work lives:** Your organization must have a heart. Foster a future-proof culture that promotes employee health, education, authentic purpose, relationships, and time to disconnect from work.

We're excited to share our discoveries and look forward to learning about how they bring value to your business. *You can WIN and futureproof your workforce in the age of disengagement.*

Chapter 2

Give Value First

Optimizing Engagement Through
Upskilling and Keeping People
Relevant, Influential, and In-Demand

Tracy Levine and Michael Levine

WIN

Tracy Levine and Michael Levine are International keynote speakers who future-proof workforces, future-proof careers and future-proof EBITDA by training corporate leaders on how to easily build a Give Value First Culture™ and optimize Employee Living Logos™.

Tracy and Michael are the Co-CEOs of Advantage Talent, Inc., a global culture engagement strategy firm.

Give Value First

All things being equal, we want to spend our time with friends and family, the people who support and enrich our quality of life. These are the people we deem "worthy" of our energy; we'll show up to help them, we'll sing their praises to anyone who will listen, and we'll share their achievements with our extended networks, both online and off. Our family and friends are where we *choose* to engage.

It's no surprise, then, that corporations have sought out ways to replicate that "friends and family" feel in the workplace, incorporating every-thing from breakroom birthday celebrations to departmental happy hours and company-wide field days. "Look how much fun we're having!" and "Look how much we care!" are the messages they want to convey. Their hope, of course, is that their employees will *choose* to engage with the company, too.

"There's just one teeny, tiny problem: they're not fooling anyone."

WIN

"Why don't the traditional engagement methods work anymore?" is a question we get asked all the time by our Fortune 500 clients. But the better question might be, *"Why should they?"*

For generations, the employer-employee dynamic was stable, understood, and upheld: employees were expected to "pay their dues" as they ascended the corporate ladder, rung by rung. The company, in turn, would reward their employees with better titles, growth opportunities, and pay increases. The big prize for company loyalty was the 401k and/or pension waiting for the employees when they retired—but these old bargains are now rare.

Corporate America ghosted its workforce.

Corporate America ghosted its workforce, first on *stability* and *long-term employment agreements,* and then on *professional growth opportunities* and meaningful investment in *training* that improves an employee's skills (a.k.a. upskilling). Changing global economic trends, automation, and accelerated disruption have increased the

14

probability that employees will be let go, laid off, or automated out of relevance. Such changes make it difficult for employees to stay emotionally engaged with their employer. It doesn't take long for a disengaged employee's trust to erode, and their loyalty will inevitably follow suit. Such disengagement and its ramifications have become so prevalent that the very definition of a successful career has begun to change.

What does a "successful" career look like today? Successful careers lead to much more than a paycheck. They lead to long-term relevance, greater quality of life, and financial well-being. A paycheck used to encompass all three, but that's no longer a given. Without those old bargains (and the engagement, trust, and loyalty they fostered), employees have little incentive to stick around. After all, a paycheck is relatively easy to find elsewhere.

Employers, meanwhile, seem unwilling (or uninterested) in trying to convince their employees to stay for the long haul. *As today's "hot" skills can quickly become the "not" skills of tomorrow*, in our rapidly changing landscape, employers are opting to transition to a "just-in-time" employee workforce. The employee must be the "just-in time solution" (available when the company needs them), the "right solution" (capable of solving the company's problem), and the "verified solution" (an acknowledged thought leader with the skills the company needs *now*). In other words, ***companies want the flexibility to hire specialized skills on demand, with no long-term commitment.***

"Only 42% of organizations surveyed are made up primarily of salaried employees." *(Deloitte 2018)*[2]

Soon, long-term employees will make up a small percentage of the workforce. In fact, a Deloitte study shows this change is already gaining momentum. As of 2017, only 19% of employers have traditional functional career paths for their employees.[2] And in 2018, a Deloitte survey revealed that only 42% of organizations are made up primarily of salaried employees.[2]   The job market is changing from a steppingstone, tenured, and a degree-based labor market to a skills-based labor market. And the skills and expertise required and desired are changing with increasing speed.

College degrees and internal training programs are often outdated by the time they are completed. Most corporate learning and development programs are not designed or equipped to train for quickly fluctuating skill-based needs. It's also difficult to predict what skills companies will need next. So companies are increasingly transferring the responsibility of upskilling to their employees.

And yet, despite all this changes, two fundamental truths endure: *people need jobs,* and *companies need a workforce.* And neither wants to settle for anything less than "success."

WIN

So how can employers attract, engage, and keep top talent in the midst of such disruption? Employees (and top prospects) are now aiming to work for companies that will add value to their professional brands. They want to be sure that each month they work for a company will make them relatively more competitive in this rapidly changing work marketplace. Engaging employees is all about your ability to *give value first*.

A *Give Value First Culture* is a company culture that:

1. Rewards upskilling and skill agility by empowering top talent to move to new responsibilities and salaries without artificial company tenure, degree, or other unnecessary barrier requirements. Employees gain skills that improve their effectiveness in their current jobs. These skills increase their ability to accept higher-value responsibilities, which then leads to increased compensation and promotion.

2. Opens pathways for employees to upskill for the broader job market instead of just for the company's internal needs. Some company leaders view upskilling as a risk that makes it difficult to hold on to employees, but the negative consequences of employee irrelevance create an even greater risk to a company's long-term success. Companies become more agile because they create a workforce that can quickly take on challenges created by competitors. Companies and employees both benefit by creating structures that encourage employees to upskill.

3. Creates opportunities for innovative tools and the execution of new ideas. As employees build skills, they become aware of new tools, ideas, and methodologies and can use them to review existing structures and processes through a new perspective. Ideas that produce extra revenue or cost savings emerge at a faster pace, managers lead skill empowered teams, and the company becomes much more competitive.

4. Fosters inclusiveness in power positions, which creates opportunities to gain experience working outside of silos and "birds of a feather" internal structures. When people with different perspectives and experience collaborate to achieve company goals, their respective soft skills improve, and their ability to produce top products for a global economy increases too.

5. Contributes to continuous professional branding. Employees are increasingly aware of their need to remain relevant, influential, and in-demand. When a company creates and maintains a *Give Value First Culture,* existing employees and new recruits recognize that they can add value to their professional brands as they add value to company stakeholders. The greater the opportunity to grow their professional brands, the more likely they are to stay engaged with the company and to add significant value to the company's brand and profit.

When a company puts these five *Give Value First Culture* elements into practice, it will uncover the secret of creating a culture that leads to stronger engagement, retention, and attraction of top talent. It will create a culture that its employees *choose* to engage with. And it may even find that employees become the best brand ambassadors, attracting other top-tier candidates to the organization.

Salesforce is an excellent example of a *Give Value First Culture*. The company actively promotes employee upskilling through its Trailhead learning program and supports external learning programs, too. Salesforce is so committed to upskilling that it has pledged to provide Salesforce credentialing to up to 500,000 American workers. The company has gained recognition as one of Forbes Most Innovative Companies, Forbes Best Workplaces for Diversity, and multiple awards that recognize Salesforce as a great place to work.

Now, consider your organization: where do you have the opportunity to incorporate the Give Value First elements in your company? For example, if you have not yet implemented a robust rewards system for upskilling, begin to map out your plan. Which parts of your company would benefit most from employee upskilling? What will an upskilled workforce add to company creativity, efficiency and effectiveness? How will it help attract top talent, and company profit? How much will your company need to invest to achieve these extra marketplace advantages? What is your plan for implementing a best-in-class upskilling environment?

Today's top talent wants to know whether a company has a Give Value First Culture, and they're not turning to the organization's messaging to find the answer—they want to know what its employees have to say.

LinkedIn operates the world's largest Internet-based professional network that includes more than 645 million members in over 200 countries and territories.[3] (It's a safe bet that your company has a presence on the site, too.) And while recruiters and hiring managers are looking at their dream candidates' LinkedIn profiles, those candidates are looking right back.

Candidates want to see whether they'll be working with leaders and peers who are successful and whether joining the company will elevate their professional brand. They want to know whether working for this company will be a good decision? Do they want to be a part of its culture?

Top Talent is also looking to see if a company's reality matches its mission statements.

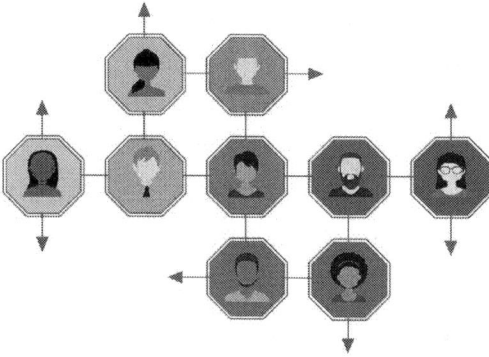

Pictures of managers eating pastries with employees, having coffee, or cheering them on for receiving meaningless kudos and awards miss the mark. They lack the authenticity today's candidates crave. Savvy candidates are bypassing the recruiting team's marketing efforts and going straight to the company's existing employees.

So is it any wonder that an employee's LinkedIn profile can now be more damaging to a company than a bad Glassdoor review? While a company can correct and address a couple of bad reviews on Glassdoor, LinkedIn brings the equivalent of the Hubble telescope to its culture and employees. If an organization isn't "walking its talk," the best candidates on the market will look elsewhere.

WIN

Google is a great example of a company that passes the LinkedIn "Hubble telescope" review, and not coincidentally, the Google diversity annual report for 2019 shows that they have experienced greater success at retaining, recruiting, and attracting top talent than many of their peers.

Read the following snippet of Google's hiring mission statement:

Google's mission is to organize the world's information and make it universally accessible and useful. When we say we want to build for everyone, we mean everyone. To do that well, we need a workforce that's more representative of the users we serve.[4]

Sounds nice enough, but how's their follow-through? Type "Google" and "vice-president" into the LinkedIn search bar, and you will see a more diverse and inclusive group than many other tech companies offer. Their hiring mission statement is not an empty marketing promise; Google is actively executing on its vision and values.

Give Value First

What's also striking about Google is the inclusiveness across age groups. They, and companies like them, understand the unbeatable value of mixing proven business experience with new and emerging hard and soft skills. New products and services get created when a company's leaders can combine agility with selective forgetting instead of clinging to what worked in the past.

Cross-age inclusive management is a strong competitive advantage and highly attractive to prospective employees. Experienced leaders can draw from their wealth of real-life business experience and quickly see when a project might be going off the rails or doesn't have the right infrastructure in place to succeed. New generations bring fresh approaches and innovative thinking that challenge old ideas, processes, and products. And the presence of both conveys to top talent that they, too, can have a seat at the table. It shows the organization has a *Give Value First Culture.*

Such inclusiveness is particularly attractive, given that the number one item that top talent wants to know is this:

WIN

"How will working for this company elevate my professional brand?" Current and potential employees want to evaluate a company's commitment to investing in employee upskilling. These employees want to be part of a culture that rewards best-in-class hard skills and soft skills because they know that these companies are more likely to grow and to create opportunities for professional growth.

A review of LinkedIn will make it easy for top-tier candidates to see whether your company's employees are upskilling. They'll also see whether the upskilling budget is confined to the company's "branded only" training, or if it includes high-value external courses or certifications.

Top talent is unlikely to be impressed if the training is exclusively internally focused, as such training doesn't always lead to meaningful professional brand enhancement. Finally, top talent can also see if upskilling creates opportunities within the company or whether employees are taking their new skills elsewhere.

As recruiters, we have asked employees why they chose to leave companies that were actively paying for external upskilling and enabling employees to build their professional brand relevance. Their answers were consistent:

- **Management has not kept up.** When managers have no framework to understand or embrace new ideas and approaches for solving problems or creating revenue, disengagement won't be far behind. It's difficult for employees who report to them to share and execute on ideas that help the company.

- **There's no opportunity or reward.** No one wants to invest their time and effort only to find that … nothing happens. No raise or promotion. Worse, they may watch as another employee (one who lacks upskilling but has "seniority" or a similarly unmeritocratic trait), moves ahead. The age of internal salary banding around tenure and titles should have already died a timely death. In a "just-in-time" hiring environment, the open market should decide who gets to lead and be paid.

"The age of internal salary banding around tenure and titles should have already died a timely death."

WIN

And yet, in our study of over 100 companies that hire top talent, we discovered that senior management often lacks upskilling, particularly if they are Gen X or baby boomers. Even millennials in senior management, hired in or promoted because of their new hot skills, show a decline in upskilling within two years. There are people in each of these age groups capable of upskilling and embracing change, so when it's clear that internal upskilling is not a C-suite initiative, top talent will see that as a red flag.

"No upskilling here. Move On."

No amount of slick marketing or social media expertise can hide a culture that isn't a *Give Value First Culture*. So, why aren't C-suite leadership teams making it a priority? The answer is simple but disappointing: their trusted advisors have not connected the dots that **every employee is a Living Logo** beyond marketing's grasp. Nor have they figured out that a *Give Value First Culture* is the most powerful tool at their disposal to attract top talent.

Give Value First

But the companies that understand and implement a *Give Value First* culture have a clear advantage. These companies build systems to reward upskilling and open pathways for career advancement. They are also investing in state-of-the-art tools and top talent, prioritizing innovation, and creating an environment that maximizes opportunities for inclusiveness and diversity. These companies have developed a culture that creates happy and supported employees and a firm foundation for these engaged employees to showcase their highly effective living logos.

WIN

Your employees are Living Logos. Executives can choose to empower their employees
to optimize their professional brands, or own the
consequences of their disengagement. Optimizing
the company's "Living Logo" is all about increasing
brand credibility and differentiating the organization through—you guessed it—a *Give Value First* culture.

But something else happens when an
organization *gives value first*: it brings the human
element back to the employer-employee dynamic. It recaptures and rebuilds the trust, loyalty, and
engagement that has fallen by the wayside in our
corporate landscape. Employees feel happy, motivated, and supported. They *choose* to engage—and
they're more likely to be a positive Living Logo.

According to Dr. William Swann, a profes-
sor of social and personality psychology at the
University of Texas at Austin, people have a
strong need for others to recognize and reinforce their self-image. This is referred to as the
self-verification theory. So why is the self-verification theory important to a company's Living
Logos? Companies that partner with employees

to showcase the employees' professional brands engage them by creating a sense of stability and control over their careers, even in the new reality of a "just-in-time" workforce. Employees take comfort in knowing that the company is dedicated to achieving a healthy balance of both corporate and team member goals.

WIN

Dr. Swann's research also suggests that once employees become engaged with a company, they are more likely to want to remain productive as members of the team. He refers to this as the *identity fusion theory*. When *identity fusion* occurs, personal and social values merge. Group members act as "family" and develop closer ties to the company and to each person within it. These employees are also more likely to be avid brand ambassadors.

So, how can companies harness the power of their Living Logos? There's a right way (and a wrong way) to do it.

• ***Content must be authentic.*** While it might be tempting to have the marketing department create a Living Logo campaign or supply employees with materials to post on their profiles and share with their respective networks, (or, worse, require them to share such items), it's a terrible idea. Brand ambassadors are most effective when they can share unique and relevant content *that matters to them* with their business networks.

• ***Content must be relevant.*** When employees post targeted content in the LinkedIn general feed with the intent of broad distribution, LinkedIn will limit distribution to other members based on its relevance to the recipient. If employees want to maximize the impact of their professional content, it is best to post to LinkedIn groups that are aligned with their specific content. It is within these professional groups that their post is more likely to receive comments. When group administrators endorse content as relevant, LinkedIn will push the content beyond that group.

• ***Content must be employee-driven.*** This is a big one, and it's where your Company's *Living Logos* and your *Give Value First Culture* will intersect in a visible way. You cannot write your employees' LinkedIn profiles for them—such inauthenticity will reek from a mile away. You can only assess what Living Logos have to say and determine where you can add more value and empower them further, boosting their impact on the companies Living Logo.

WIN

Start by taking a close look at your team's LinkedIn profiles from an outsider's perspective. Will they see that your team has developed in-demand skills, that they are learning, upskilling, and growing professionally? Refer back to the elements of a *Give Value First Culture* and look for opportunities to boost your employees' *Living Logos*.

Then turn your eye to your profile. Are you an accomplished mentor endorsing and recommending your work colleagues? Are you receiving endorsements and recommendations from them? Do you share original content that is relevant to your key customers and to potential top candidates? Are you NOT spamming the feed with marketing department generated content?

Corporate Leaders should be the cornerstone of a great Employee Living Logo. As a leader, you will see opportunities to improve your Living Logo. As you take action, it is always best to remember the three goals of accessibility, relevance, and thought leadership. You'll be on your way to creating the influence needed to become a thought leader that top talent, employees, colleagues, and customers seek to partner with.

34

Give Value First

The path to engagement is clear and accessible. Current and future employees want a *Give Value First Culture* at work. Companies that are committed to rewarding upskilling and facilitating professional growth have a distinct advantage in attracting top talent and keeping them engaged. Add to that a workplace that includes openness to innovation, diversity and inclusiveness, and a commitment to employee brand optimization, and you'll find an environment where employees thrive and attract top candidates.

The disruption in today's employer-employee dynamic is a challenge, no doubt, but the outlook isn't all doom and gloom. In many ways, we're seeing a tremendous opportunity for companies to set themselves apart by adopting a *Give Value First Culture* and empowering their employees to build the successful careers they want.

"The Best CULTURES Win! Mastering the Art of Employee Engagement is about Creating A Give Value First Culture."

WIN

We're not talking about window dressing, fads, or buzz words. We're talking about making your company into a place where people want to be and will choose to spend their time. Having a "prestige" name is no longer the advantage it once was, and the door has been opened for a broader group of companies to compete in the war for talent and engagement—and those that embrace the *Give Value First Culture* and harness the power of the *Living Logo* will **WIN**.

"Attracting and engaging top talent and next-gen leaders is no longer just an HR initiative. It's a business imperative, and everyone must participate."

Tracy Levine and Michael Levine

Chapter 3

Engaged At The Door

Optimizing Productivity Per Square Foot through dynamic workspaces

Michelle Galvani and Jenny O'Donnell

WIN

*Michelle Galvani and Jenny O'Donnell help
companies rethink their workspaces
to drive operational efficiencies and
foster employee engagement
to optimize Productivity Per Square Foot™.*

*Michelle is the Executive Managing Director and
Jenny is Executive Director of Wildmor Advisors, a
global commercial real estate advisory firm.*

Engaged at the Door

We can all conjure up an image of the disengaged employee; the movie Office Space probably comes to mind. Mike Judge, who wrote and directed the 1999 film, based it off his experiences working as an engineer in Silicon Valley in the 1980s. The satire depicts the original "cube culture" with an endless maze of 6-foot-tall gray workstations and beige filing cabinets sitting under fluorescent lights, with the only pop of color being a bright red stapler.

This cult sensation forever changed attitudes about how we look at cubicle life. It left an indelible image of how disconnected the built environment can be to the human element. The movie highlights how a poorly designed workspace with subpar technology creates obstacles and headaches that ultimately drive employees to disengagement.

In real life, the problems aren't so obvious. Many workspaces look fine at first, but may actually have flaws that employees silently cope with. Why? Few companies pay close attention to office design. Think about it: Even if your employees knew about a design flaw, would they come to you and say, "Hey, we need to tear down this wall and add collaborative space in our area". Or would they bring in their tools and knock down their cube wall letting natural light in like Peter Gibbons did in the movie?

Most of us just deal with what's available. When companies do think about office space, it's usually just because they need to expand or because their lease is expiring. That's exactly what happened to a client we worked with at a custom software development and technical staffing company.

Our client came to us with a simple goal: renew the lease at a lower rental rate. The space was well appointed with a front lobby that had an undeniable WOW factor. The client had upgraded some areas a few years earlier, so it made sense to renew. But there was one big problem: Employees desperately needed more meeting rooms.

The programmers were separated by 6-foot-tall workstations that didn't allow for collaboration. They routinely juggled several client projects, with teams of four to six developers working together. But they only had a couple of small meeting rooms available. That meant teams had no collaborative space and a lot of useless cubes.

This situation was frustrating employees and hindering productivity.

We tabled the renewal discussion and started tackling the productivity challenge. This meant gathering critical data including insights from employees about what they needed to do their jobs more efficiently.

Then we flipped the script and evaluated how other locations would impact the team's commute. We also reviewed the technology infrastructure of each building to ensure the best computing experience and focused on something that's often overlooked: whether there's reliable cell phone coverage. We measured everything against one essential litmus test: "How much will this improve our client's *Productivity Per Square Foot*?"

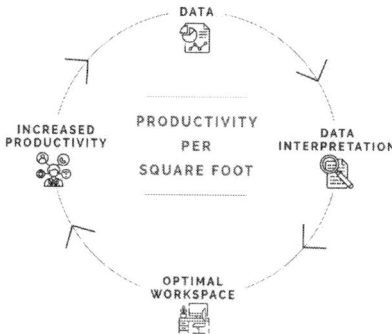

DATA

PRODUCTIVITY PER SQUARE FOOT

DATA INTERPRETATION

OPTIMAL WORKSPACE

INCREASED PRODUCTIVITY

WIN

The best solution for the client was found in a different building. It had superb technological infrastructure and stellar amenities, including a fitness center, restaurants within walking distance, and a tunnel connecting the building to the city's public train station. Better yet, the space could be customized to fit the team's needs, allowing for collaboration, creativity, and better productivity.

The outcome was extraordinary — a complete transformation that elevated the team's energy and enthusiasm. The "first impression area" went from a lobby with great views to a community-centric space with inviting couches, a farm table where team members and guests can interact, and a well stocked kitchen. The programmers had plenty of group spaces, including workstations configured for collaboration, private conference rooms, semi-private meeting areas separated by a curtain, specialized furniture, and a coffee bar. Each space was meticulously designed to suit any type of internal meeting, client presentations, and interviews.

The client told us many employees shed tears of joy when seeing their new workspace at the unveiling party. We credit our client, who recognized how important it was to go through our process to understand what the team needed to perform at its very best.

This experience highlights the need for companies to be nimble and open-minded. Our client could have just signed another five-year lease in the old building. Many companies do. But by taking a step back and assessing the workspace needs of the employees, this company greatly increased its *Productivity Per Square Foot*.

WIN

Why do so many employers fall short with their workspaces?

Often, employers just aren't aware of the problems. Like our client in the example above, they might have an office with nice views and a good location, giving them a false sense of security on the quality of their workspaces. But many of those workspaces are underperforming — leading employees to underperform, too.

What causes employers to overlook crucial workspace problems?

1. IT'S NOT A PRIORITY: Most companies focus on office space when their leases are about to expire or when they need to expand. That's usually just once every few years. This creates an "out of sight, out of mind" situation.

2. LIMITED INPUT: Managing a company's workspace is typically a secondary role to whoever gets assigned the responsibility. These people are usually in finance, HR, or operations. Because the workspace impacts every department, each

department should be represented in the decision-making process. Most of the time, leadership will choose not to involve everyone in order to mitigate work disruptions. But the cost of not involving department thought leaders potentially results in a workspace that does not meet the needs of each department or employee.

3. SHORT-SIGHTED EVALUATION: The go to evaluation has always been focused around the cost per square foot and total rentable square feet. According to CoreNet Global, an international real estate group, the average square feet of office space per person has fallen from 225 in 2010 to 150 in 2013.[5] This trend of dwindling space is expected to continue due to cost savings. But by slashing these costs, companies can end up paying far more in terms of lost productivity and employee disengagement.

Why do trendy office upgrades fail to engage top talent and next-gen leaders?

One of the costliest mistakes happens when company leadership designs or modifies their space according to what's trendy and ignores how their employees use the space. This oversight can plunge engagement levels. To see this in action, just look at the open office plan.

Silicon Valley firms were the first to champion open workspaces. They eliminated private offices, deeming them outdated symbols of corporate hierarchy. Instead, they clustered team members communally to foster collaboration and innovation. But the plan backfired.

In 2018, Harvard Business School researchers analyzed the impact of an open workspace on collaboration. They used groundbreaking techniques to measure the effects, including electronic badges and microphones to record employee interactions and track email. Instead of increased engagement, the open office layout triggered a withdrawal response. Face-to-face interactions decreased by almost 70%, and electronic messages increased by 50%.[6] Even though this cutting-edge idea was inherently flawed, companies in almost every major city copied it — without a clear understanding of the negative effects on employees.

Engaged at the Door

If your space isn't helping your team excel, it's costing you. If the workspace hinders productivity, stifles creativity, or suppresses a sense of wellness and community, it's costing you. And if it's driving away your top performers or prospective talent, it's costing you even more.

What's your Productivity Per Square Foot?

Productivity Per Square Foot is the measurement of increased engagement motivated by a good workplace experience. It is positioning your team in the right place to achieve top tier performance and a sustained winning culture. But maximizing Productivity Per Square Foot often requires a complete paradigm shift in how office spaces are evaluated, implemented, and managed.

Here's how to get started:

Assemble the right team: Every department is impacted by the built environment. So it's essential to have every department represented in the decision-making process.

WIN

Collect data: This includes a deep dive into the organizational structure and drilling down to the employee level. We leverage diverse cutting-edge data and predictive analytics to empower our clients to make successful decisions. While it may not be feasible to make a change in every location, it's important to look at how the company operates as a whole to ensure proper alignment to the culture. Develop a strategic plan: Determine short-, mid-, and long-term implementation objectives and Productivity Per Square Foot goals.

Benchmark: Develop customized key performance indicators (KPI's) to benchmark and measure results.

Implement in phases: The plan should include action items that can be implemented at different times to allow flexibility and ensure the most significant impact.

Perform ongoing assessments: Due to rapidly changing workplace dynamics, workspaces should be revaluated on a continuous basis and adjusted when necessary.

What questions should companies be asking?

• Does your built and virtual environment reflect and support the company culture?

• How does your workplace support your employees' wellbeing?

• Does your building/location align with your company's needs? For example, are there common areas with a wireless connection to allow untethered working? Do you have electric car charging stations, green space, or a fitness facility?

• What type of reaction does your workspace evoke from interviewees or visitors?

• What is the energy level of your employees?

• How would you rate your workspace in terms of maximizing productivity and attracting talent? Is it agile?

51

WIN

• When was the last time team members were asked to evaluate the way they work and what improvements could be made to support them?

• Is your work environment adapted to fit your evolving workforce and meet new competitive challenges? Does it foster innovation? Is it equipped with the right technology?

• How can remote workers connect to the physical workspace?

• Will your building's technology infrastructure and geographical area support your business going forward?

• How are you leveraging your built environment to recruit and retain top talent?

What do employees want?

Asking the right questions and evaluating social data to uncover what's working, what could work better, and where your environment is falling short is the first step towards turning a liability into an asset. So, if you've never considered how your employees use their space or how they'd like to use their space, now is a great time to find out.

In a recent survey, the Harvard Business Review[7] looked into "What Employees Want Most from their Workspaces," and here is what they found:

1. Air Quality
2. Comfortable Light
3. Water Quality
4. Comfortable Temperatures
5. Connection to Nature
6. Comfortable Acoustics
7. Healthy Food Options
8. Fitness Facilities
9. Tech-Based Health Tools

While these things might top the survey list, there are undoubtedly other factors that employees are looking for in a workspace. We know because we asked (and listened). Employees want a physical space that allows them to recharge and feel productive.

WIN

They prefer a flexible environment that offers them the freedom to choose from a variety of settings for different activities and purposes. These areas must be easily accessible and equipped with the proper high-speed internet and other technologies in order for them to get their work done efficiently. In addition, office park amenities are becoming an extension of the office, allowing the untethered workforce to take advantage of training rooms, fitness facilities, cafes, walking trails, and WIFI-enabled outdoor communal areas.

Simply put, employees are more attracted to companies that focus on an employee-centric view of workplace wellness. If your company focuses on your employees' needs, you will have greater productivity, engagement, and retention. And your employees can share their positive experiences with potential candidates.

Workspace as Agile as your Workforce

Just like your employees, your workspace needs to be dynamic and ready for the future. The use of prefabricated modular walls, room dividers and moveable furniture can be rearranged on demand, allowing your workforce to be productive and efficient while future-proofing your environment.

Even better, there is no need to wait to experiment with a modular system within a traditional workspace as prefabricated modular systems can be installed within a matter of days. And they don't just save time and money. They're also reusable, recyclable and virtually dust free, which benefits the air quality.

What improvements will have an immediate impact?

No matter your industry, space constraints, or budget, these steps can instantly boost wellness and productivity:

• Add a filtered water system and provide eco-friendly water bottles for each employee. Your health-conscious (and eco-conscious) employees will love it, and it could lower your health insurance costs.

• Keep a stash of healthy snacks. Providing healthy snacks such as fruit and vegetables has shown

to reduce stress, improve focus, and increase productivity.

• Provide recycling bins. Use recycled and com-
postable plates, utensils, cups, and paper towels
so everyone can support sustainability. This also
shows that the company cares about the environment, which is especially important to younger
generations.

• Let in natural light. If possible, bring in more
natural light or add directional light that supports
circadian rhythm. Your brain reacts to the amount
of light it receives through the eyes, and when it is
dark outside, your brain gets a signal that it is time
to feel tired. With a brighter workspace, the employee is more alert.

• Provide blue light filters. This is important because blue light (generated by computer screens)
can suppress the production of melatonin (a
sleep-inducing hormone), so filtering it out can
help you sleep better. It will also reduce digital eye
strain, so your eyes won't feel so tired by the end
of the day.

Engaged at the Door

• Design areas that allow for specific tasks. This includes collaborative workspaces, training facilities, and telephone rooms.

• Install an air filtration system. Removing breathable pollutants and moisture from the air creates a refreshing, clean feeling and a more comfortable atmosphere. Cleaner air also means healthier employees and fewer sick days.

• Incorporate live plants. They're a cost-effective alternative to an air filtration system. Plus, they bring nature indoors, reduce stress, create a healthier environment and can even absorb sound.

• Reconsider your paint color. The right color can influence employee behavior, mood, productivity, and attitude. Green inspires creativity; blue is relaxing and powerful; yellow promotes fun and spontaneous thoughts, and white is airy and fresh. No matter your color preference, make sure it invokes the feeling you want.

• Offer ergonomic workstations in terms of seating

and sit/stand desks. Both offer health benefits and mood boosters. Find ways to provide these to your remote workforce, too. It will reinforce that they are part of the team and show that you want them to have the best experience, even at home.

• Improve connectivity. Make sure that your workspace is equipped with the technology to allow your employees to work effectively. This will also ensure that remote/mobile workers will have the platforms to stay connected with the rest of the team.

• Choose a location that complements the company culture. We have worked with so many companies that are in the wrong setting. Tech companies housed in a building more suited toward service providers such as attorneys or accountants will probably have a tough time attracting and retaining top talent.

Your Transformation Can Start Today

Leveraging your built environment to improve the employee experience is one of the most underutilized advantages in business today. The return on investment potential is undoubtedly higher than any other investment a company can make and could be the difference between a company moving forward or being left behind. So why aren't more companies paying attention to this? The short answer seems to be that company leadership has enough on their plate as it is: cybersecurity, geopolitical and regulation concerns, keeping up with the speed of technology, and, at the top of the list, vying against their competitors for top talent. Relocation and renovation aren't cheap; we get it. But, you don't have to do everything at once (in fact, it's probably better if you don't). Small changes can have a big impact on your employees. And the sooner you show them you care, the better.

Can you afford to invest the time and resources into employee engagement and the war on talent and not have the built environment support it?

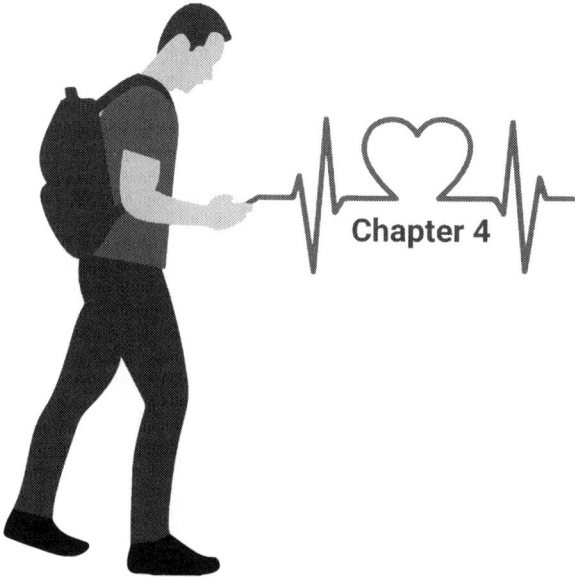

Chapter 4

Giving HEART™

Optimizing Engagement by
Supporting Healthy and Impactful
Employee Work Lives

Chris Butsch

WIN

Chris Butsch is a global keynote speaker helping leaders implement HEART™ for heightened engagement.

Giving HEART

It's 5:57 pm in Haarlem, a suburb of Amsterdam.

In the offices of Heldergroen, a prominent Dutch design and branding firm, senior strategist Marjolein Doets notices the warm glow of the sunset reflecting off her monitor.

The workday is over.

Suddenly but gently, every desk in the office starts rising to the ceiling, computers and all.

As the shared desks elevate above the employees' heads, Ms. Doets looks around at her coworkers, now sitting comically deskless. They share a tongue-in-cheek grin.

This never gets old, she thinks.

WIN

House of the Rising Office

Though it (literally) separates employees from their work each night, Heldergroen's famous "disappearing office" didn't start as a work-life balance tool. Rather, it began as a practical way to create more space.

To boost wellness and collaboration, employees requested a multi-use space for yoga, meditation, and family-style meals. But leasing more office space in Amsterdam would be far too expensive. Instead, together with CEO Sander Veenendaal, they innovated a more cost-effective solution:

Why not elevate the desks to the ceiling and simply use the space we already pay for?

As a team, the employees and leadership did just that. By rigging the same wires used in theatrical productions to hidden motors and pulleys, Heldergroen implemented the "disappearing office" for less than $22,000.

Employees were delighted by their "new"

space. But Veenendaal saw more opportunity for increased employee wellness and engagement.

Each night, regardless of workload or client demands, Veenendaal activates the disappearing office at 6 pm sharp. Computers, coffee mugs, and work of any kind stay out-of-reach until the next morning. Heldergroen employees are then totally free to share a potluck meal, practice yoga, or simply go home.

Veenendaal heavily credits the disappearing office with an immediate and enduring surge in productivity, engagement, and retention. While his competitors continue to poach and shuffle talent like Silicon Valley tech giants (at enormous expense), Heldergroen employees happily stay put.

"There are firms in downtown Amsterdam that offer more prestige and money," he said. "But each morning, my employees bike right past them to work here."

The power of the disappearing office isn't in the mechanism; it's in the message. *Go home. Be with your family. Work will be here in the morning.*

To Veenendaal, "the disappearing office is how we remind ourselves: life first, work second."

WIN

Employees Engage with Employers Who Give HEART™

What makes employees feel engaged?

We know the answer isn't money. If it was, the most lucrative industries would also have the most engaged employees (when in fact the opposite is often true — there's only a 2% overlap between pay and job satisfaction).[8]

No, it must be something else. Certain companies around the world offer their employees something beyond their salaries that supercharges their engagement.

What's the secret to preventing disengagement?

To find out, I spent over 1,000 hours researching and infiltrating the world's most engaged workforces. I discovered these companies win engagement not just by providing a good salary, but by giving HEART™.

Giving HEART

HEART™ is a combination of:

- **Health:** mental and physical well-being

- **Education:** growth through feedback, mentoring, and continuous learning

- **Authenticity:** purpose, meaning, and transparency from leadership

- **Relationships:** healthy connections with family, friends, and coworkers

- **Time:** flexibility, vacation, and time spent disconnected from work

WIN

HEART™ is measurable, attainable, and reveals why certain engagement solutions work while others disappoint. For example...

HEART™ Explains Why Remote Work Spikes Engagement

Employees want to be able to work remotely, and they're more engaged when they can. According to Gallup:

• All employees who spend at least some (but not all) of their time working remotely have higher engagement than those who never work remotely.[9]

• 37% of employees say they would switch to a job that would allow at least part-time remote work.[10]

• Remote work improves productivity and retention by 25%.[11]

To reap the benefits, companies are quickly adopting remote work policies. In 2020, half of American employees have remote work privileges.

By 2030, more than 90% will.

What's more important than offering your employees remote work privileges is understanding *why* it works. Sure, employees working 60% remotely can save $8,000 annually in commuting costs.[12] But we already know that money doesn't increase engagement.

Rather, employees are more engaged with remote work because it gives them HEART™:

• *Health:* A 2012 study in the American Journal of Preventive Medicine linked commuting to cardiovascular disease, obesity, and lower mental health.[13] Naturally, 82% of remote workers report lower stress and greater happiness.[14]

• *Education:* Employees who work remotely 60-80% of the time are the most likely of all employees to strongly agree they have opportunities to learn and grow.[15]

• *Authenticity:* In Gallup surveys, remote workers give their employers higher scores on "mission and purpose," indicating that "remote workers may feel more connected to their companies, despite physical distance."[15]

• *Relationships:* Employees who work 60-80% remotely are the most likely of all employees to strongly agree that they have a best friend at work, meaning they're more than twice as likely to stay engaged.[16]

• *Time:* the average commute time in America is 25.4 minutes each way.[17] The employee who works from home three days a week saves 132.6 hours per year.

Since remote work gives so much HEART™, *how do you think employees react when their employers try to take that privilege away?*

Following in the footsteps of several other Fortune 500 companies, Bank of New York Mellon announced plans in 2018 to scale back remote work options. Employees reacted in strong defense of their remote work privileges, and the company put the plans on indefinite hold.

Good save. BNY Mellon almost learned the hard way that engagement and HEART™ are inextricably linked. When those other companies repealed remote work, absenteeism increased by up to 60%.[18]

The moral of the story is this: Don't mess with your employees' HEART™.

HEART™ Also Reveals Why Top Talent and Next-Gen Leaders Quit

Here's a question I often hear from clients:
"Why did one of my best employees just quit?"

As part of my response, I tell the story of my friend Lizzy.

Lizzy, 36, was initially thrilled by her new promotion. Due to the stress of the job, very few people make it to the rank of Application Director (AD). The promotion would include a larger office, more challenging projects, and an extra digit on her paycheck. Sweet.

To ensure success in her new role, Lizzy

began observing her company's application direc-tors like a corporate Jane Goodall.

What she saw distressed her.

She described ADs as constantly stressed out. They had bloodshot eyes and were exhausted to the point of hysteria, like vampires raising seven toddlers.

Across the board, ADs looked miserable. "When does the stress let up?" she asked one. He let out a non-answer and slunked away, seemingly relegated to his fate.

Three months later, Lizzy began working for a competitor. It offered her less compensation in a more expensive city, but she enthusiastically ac-cepted.

"Here, the managers are happy, healthy, and have good work-life balance," she said. "I think that alone says so much about the company's culture and priorities."

To her former employer, Lizzy was the ideal employee: engaged and driven, with strong potential as a highly effective leader. When she left the company, they were surely vexed:

Giving HEART

Why would an engaged employee not only reject a promotion, but suddenly quit?

A look at the problem through the lens of HEART™ reveals why.

By nature, top talent and next-gen leaders have good foresight. Regardless of how engaged they are now, if they foresee a dip in HEART™, they're more likely to disengage or even quit.

This is exactly what happened to Lizzy. She initially got excited about the money, but then saw clear signs of lower HEART™ benefits:

• *Health:* ADs were visibly stressed and sleep deprived
• *Education:* ADs received no additional training or formal mentoring
• *Authenticity:* ADs seemed disillusioned by the company mission
• *Relationships:* Due to increased travel, ADs spent less time at home
• *Time:* ADs received 5 more vacation days, but seemed to work every night and weekend.

WIN

In the end, the dip in HEART™ wasn't worth the money. It almost never is.

Lizzy naturally gravitated toward a company that gave more HEART™, despite the drop in pay. She's just one example, but it happens every day.

If you want to keep your top talent and next-gen leaders, just remember: *If you lower HEART™, talent departs.*

How do you know if your company has HEART™ problems?

• Have you recently lost a next-gen leader?
• Are you struggling to attract top talent?
• Is absenteeism up on Mondays?
• Do people quit immediately after performance reviews?
• Is your Glassdoor score below average (3.9)?

If you answered yes to any of the above issues, you may have a HEART™ problem.

To fix, let's look at traditional engagement solutions you might already be using.

By tweaking how you use existing tools, you can increase engagement without having to implement new solutions.

Traditional Engagement Solutions Fail When They Don't Give HEART™

Have you purchased an engagement solution that led to disappointment? You're not alone. Since 2009, American employers have spent billions trying to engage employees. The five most common solutions are:

- Gamification
- Feedback Collection
- Learning and Development
- Perks
- Wellness Programs

Have these solutions paid off? Well, in the same span of time these solutions became popular:

- Employee engagement has decreased 2%

WIN

> • Disengagement has ballooned into a trillion-dollar problem
> • Half of employees under 40 plan to quit their job within two years.[19]

Why aren't traditional engagement solutions working? If you've already paid to implement a traditional engagement solution, how can you modify it to see better results?

• *Gamification* can improve productivity when baked into a culture that supports competition or when used to clarify work objectives. But these gains are often short-lived.

80% of workplace gamification efforts fail to improve engagement because they try to squeeze productivity out of employees without giving HEART™.[20] When one pharmacy IT giant rolled out an employee leaderboard, employees felt pressured and "overly monitored," leading to a spike in turnover. Hotel staff at one well-known resort company call gamification "the electronic whip."

Rather than gamify *productivity*, call center outsourcing firm LiveOps gamified *training*, slashing onboarding time by 80%.[21] Deloitte used the same strategy to boost return traffic to Deloitte Leadership Academy by 37%.[22]

Both LiveOps and Deloitte used gamification to give HEART™ through Education. Rather than "whipping" employees into increased output, they fostered continuous learning, winning engagement in return.

• *Learning and Development.* 59% of high-engagement companies offer employees stipends for online learning. 30% spend $2,500 or more per employee on continuous learning.[23] Yes, L&D can increase engagement, but only when it gives HEART™.

In a surprise gesture, one well-known restaurant chain began offering employees a free course called Understanding Customer Needs. The "class" was two hours of how to upsell the chain's new line of desserts. Because the class didn't give HEART™, employees felt bamboozled and the company suffered a 20% spike in disengagement.

Like with gamification, L&D opportunities

work best when they prioritize Education over output. 62% of companies that teach creative writing, mindfulness, public speaking, and other general skills saw an immediate and measurable increase in engagement.[24]

• **_Feedback Collection_** is a slippery slope. Companies often spend millions collecting feedback. "Then they make a fatal mistake," said Laszlo Bock, former SVP of people operations at Google.

They ask for their employees' Time to fill out a survey, but do little or nothing with the feedback, lowering their Authenticity. This is nothing short of a HEART™ attack!

"When you don't act on what your people have told you are the most important issues they face, your company's culture doesn't just stay the same. It gets much, much worse," Bock said.[25]

Feedback collection is an excellent way to identify your employees' HEART™ wishes and needs. Just be sure to act on what they say (or at the very least acknowledge it).

• **Perks** like catered lunches, outdoor retreats, and extra PTO can widely vary in their effects on engagement. A 2016 Glass door survey found 57% of job candidates list benefits and perks as a top consideration.[26] But it is important to distinguish *which* perks and *why*.

Not surprisingly, the perks that increase engagement the most are those that give the most HEART™. Glassdoor found that employees valued these five perks the highest because of their "life-changing potential":[27]

1. *Reebok:* paid exercise time and free CrossFit classes (Health)
2. *Starbucks:* tuition reimbursement for online bachelor's degrees (Education)
3. *Timberland:* 40 hours of PTO for volunteer efforts of their choice (Authenticity)
4. *IKEA:* four months of paid parental leave (Relationships)
5. *Deloitte:* A 3-month to 6-month sabbatical at 40% pay (Time)

WIN

Do the perks at your office give HEART™?

• *Wellness Programs* fail 90% to 95% of the time because they prioritize accountability and cost-savings over HEART™.[28] Step counters, leaderboards, and biometric scans are just expensive measuring sticks. FitBit's valid, yet coldly Orwellian website copy illustrates:

Business leaders recognize the burden of rising healthcare costs to their companies and their employees.[29]

When employers implement wellness solutions specifically to drive healthcare costs down, they typically end up disappointed. These solutions are superficial at best, and invasive and punitive at worst. Wellness programs work as engagement tools not when they poke, prod, and punish, but when they give HEART™.

Multimedia finance company Motley Fool connects employees who've never met in collaborative fitness classes. Employees at Earth Friendly Products cultivate an organic garden together. Zappos has recess. These non-traditional wellness programs work because of one simple difference: employees are improving Health, Education, Authenticity, and even Relationships, and their employers receive engagement in return.

Does Your Company Give HEART™?

Heldergroen isn't a perfect company. Employees can't work remotely, and many have long commutes. Most would make more money if they defected to the competition.

Yet they're still happy, engaged, productive, and loyal.

By implementing the disappearing office and giving HEART™ in clever ways, Veenendaal received an immediate, measurable, and enduring spike in employee engagement. With a focus on HEART™, Heldergroen continues to out-recruit, outperform, and outmaneuver the competition.

The impact of HEART™ cannot be ignored. Companies prioritizing profits over HEART™ are already struggling to recruit, retain, and engage talent. As long as they neglect their HEART™, their problems will only get worse.

WIN

Meanwhile, companies like Heldergroen, IKEA, Reebok, Starbucks, Bain, and Timberland continue to thrive as a *direct* result of how much HEART™ they give. There is not a single company among the Fortune 100 Best Companies to Work For™ that doesn't give HEART™. And Fortune 500 companies neglecting their HEART™ are sliding off the list.

Disengagement is an urgent crisis, but we're already seeing a tremendous opportunity for employers to get ahead by embracing HEART™.

Companies that take care of their HEART™ today are the ones that will survive and thrive tomorrow.

Chapter 5

Time to WIN!

Companies that future-proof their workforce today will WIN tomorrow

Tracy Levine and Michael Levine
Michelle Galvani and Jenny O'Donnell
Chris Butsch

Time to WIN!

Our sincerest thanks for reading **WIN**.

We started the research on how to "Future-Proof your Workforce in the age of disengagement" and shared with you highlights of what we learned. We don't want to be – and shouldn't be- the only ones talking collaboratively about solving the employee engagement crisis. And the Business Network Pledge is just words if leaders and professionals at all levels of an organization don't act.

"We share a fundamental commitment to all of our stakeholders... we commit to investing in our employees."
BUSINESS ROUNDTABLE, STATEMENT ON THE PURPOSE OF A CORPORATION, AUGUST 2019

Complex issues need comprehensive solutions that are simple to execute. It's your job now to make the ideas in WIN come to life and talk with your colleagues at work, leaders in your community, and engage a variety of subject matter experts. Write about the ideas in the book on social media, embrace them, or, better yet, take the ideas to the next level. That's how corporate culture starts to change – conversation by conversation.

On the following pages, we have included 15 Questions to get the discussion started. Writing your thoughts down in the space provided is the first step to taking action.

Give Value First

1. Have Tracy Levine and Michael Levine persuaded you that employee expectations have changed and that in the past few years companies who targeted Employee Engagement have overwhelmingly missed their engagement goals? Do you agree that companies need an effective Employee Engagement system that improves the performance of the company and improves employee careers? Why or why not?

2. How has the change in the paradigm of the employer/employee relationship, and the related erosion of employee trust impacted your company's economic performance? Have you failed in your efforts to retain and/or hire some in-demand candidates?

WIN

3. What is your company doing to become the strongest magnet for top talent? How often does your company conduct a professional brand value improvement review for each employee? What tools are being used by your company to measure improvements to the professional brand value of each of your employees? How are you rewarding your employees as they improve their professional brand value (additional responsibilities, compensation, promotions, and other incentives and benefits)?

4. What steps are you taking to maintain an environment where ideas for improving corporate culture and economic performance are both rewarded? Does your company strategy for promotion and compensation include an element of focus on brand value-add based on diversity of thought? What steps are you taking to ensure that a diverse employee group fills company senior leadership roles?

5. Are some employees frustrated because they have been unable to gain 'buy-in' for state-of-the-art tools to improve external and internal customer experience? Is this frustration causing your company to lose top talent employees? What is your company doing to support and reward employee upskilling? Have you implemented a customized upskilling strategy for each employee? Are upskilling achievements of executive leaders and other managers measured and rewarded?

Time to WIN!

Engaged at the Door

1. Have Michelle Galvani and Jenny O'Donnell demonstrated to you that there is a direct link between the physical space and employee Productivity Per Square Foot? Does your workspace engage your employees at the door and provide the necessary environment for optimal performance? How is this measured?

WIN

2. Do you know what your employees want, and value, in order to enhance retention and engagement? Does your space foster innovation and can it adapt to the evolving workforce? Is technology universal throughout the space? How often is this evaluated? What key performance indicators are being used to measure this?

3. What data are you using, how is it being collected? Are you certain you are achieving the highest level of data integrity and that the data is being interpreted by someone who is properly trained? Based on this data, are they able to determine how the employees work within the space and, whether or not, their needs are being met?

WIN

4. Who has responsibility for the physical asset(s) and are they involved in the development and implementation of the organization's strategic plan?

5. Have you been persuaded as to the importance of the workspace reflecting and supporting the company culture and that this goes beyond simply posting a mission statement on the wall? Does your workspace evoke a feeling of the company's mission, vision, and values? What measures have been taken to ensure that your remote/virtual employees are connected and engaged with the organization? Do you have key performance indicators in place to monitor their success?

WIN

Giving HEART™

1. Has Chris Butsch persuaded you that a renewed focus on employee Health, Education, Authenticity, Relationships, and Time is essential to sustainable engagement? Why or why not?

2. Google "[your company] GLASSDOOR" to find out how current and former employees rate various aspects of your company culture.

a. Is your company's overall score higher or lower than average (3.9)? Why?

b. What are the reported pros and cons of working at your company? What do they reveal about your company's HEART™?

c. Click REVIEWS and sort by HIGHEST and LOWEST. What do these reviews reveal about your company's HEART™? Where are some opportunities for improvement?

d. Visit the Glassdoor pages of two of your competitors. What do their ratings reveal about their HEART™? In which of the five aspects of HEART™ do they seem to have a competitive advantage? How can you take that advantage back?

WIN

3. How has a lack of HEART™ affected your company's economic performance? How has giving HEART™ improved it?

4. What steps is your company doing to improve engagement through HEART™?

WIN

5. How is your company showcasing HEART™ internally for improved retention? How is your company advertising HEART™ externally for improved recruitment?

WIN Assessments

Applying What You Learned

To help make this book actionable, we've created a three-part assessment to evaluate where your company is in the workforce future-proofing process.

WIN

Assess: Your Company's level of Employees' Career Engagement

Review each statement and select the number that reflects how much you agree or disagree with the statement.

1. Our company uses an effective system for meeting (or exceeding) our Employees' Career Engagement Goals.

Strongly disagree 1 * 2 * 3 * 4 * 5 * 6 * 7 Strongly Agree

2. Employee Trust is high in our company and we consistently hire the most In-Demand candidates.

Strongly disagree 1 * 2 * 3 * 4 * 5 * 6 * 7 Strongly Agree

3. Our employees know that active upskilling is supported, recognized, and rewarded by the corporate leadership team.

Strongly disagree 1 * 2 * 3 * 4 * 5 * 6 * 7 Strongly Agree

4. Our company is recognized by Top Talent as 'the company of choice' for achieving their professional brand value goals.

Strongly disagree 1 * 2 * 3 * 4 * 5 * 6 * 7 Strongly Agree

5. Our executive leaders maintain a culture that focuses on diversity of thought and because of this focus, our employees frequently contribute innovative value-add ideas.

Strongly disagree 1 * 2 * 3 * 4 * 5 * 6 * 7 Strongly Agree

Calculate your company score: Add the number of points from each answer to arrive at your total score.

If your total is 10 or less, your Employee Career Engagement level is low and your company is at a competitive disadvantage. You are likely experiencing serious career engagement, retention, and recruiting challenges. There is significant danger of failure to meet sustainable profitability goals.

WIN

Potential remedial steps – invest time and other resources in your employees or they may try to find another company that will.

If your score is 11-25, your Employee Career Engagement level is average and you are likely doing something well. You may be seeing some signs that you are being disrupted by competitors with a higher score. Existing employees may be at risk of departure, and recruiting will likely become more difficult as candidates for roles notice company characteristics that may cause them pain.

If your score is 26-35, your Employee Career Engagement level is high and you're approaching best in class. You know that complacency is not an option, so continue to do what you do well, and always be looking for opportunities to improve Employee Career Engagement as your competition works to WIN your best people.

Assess: Your Company's level of Workspace Engagement

Review each statement and select the number that reflects how much you agree or disagree with the statement.

1. Employees, employee candidates or guests entering our workspace experience the essence of our company culture.

Strongly disagree 1 * 2 * 3 * 4 * 5 * 6 * 7 Strongly Agree

2. We utilize robust data to gain insights and have an in-depth understanding of our employees' workstyles and offer workspace that supports the diverse needs.

Strongly disagree 1 * 2 * 3 * 4 * 5 * 6 * 7 Strongly Agree

3. Our company recognizes the demands of the business are changing and our success is tied to our employees' ability to be innovative and nimble.

WIN

As such, we ensure that our workspace is agile and adjustments are made as needed in order to support and advance our employees productivity.

Strongly disagree 1 * 2 * 3 * 4 * 5 * 6 * 7 Strongly Agree

4. We place an emphasis on our workspace supporting the health and wellness of our employees including the best air quality, drinking water, lighting, a fitness center, walking trails, etc.

Strongly disagree 1 * 2 * 3 * 4 * 5 * 6 * 7 Strongly Agree

5. Our building offers the technology infrastructure to support our digital transformation, fastest computing abilities, superior wireless capabilities, etc.

Strongly disagree 1 * 2 * 3 * 4 * 5 * 6 * 7 Strongly Agree

Calculate your company score: Add the number of points from each answer to arrive at your total score.

If your total is 10 or less, your Workplace Engagement level is low and your company is at a competitive disadvantage. You are likely experiencing serious engagement, retention, and recruiting challenges. There is significant danger of failure to meet sustainable profitability goals. Potential remedial steps – invest in Workplace upgrades for your employees or they may try to find another company that will.

If your score is 11-25, your Workplace Engagement level is average and you are likely doing something well. You may be seeing some signs that you are being disrupted by competitors with a higher score. Existing employees may be at risk of departure, and recruiting will likely become more difficult as candidates for roles notice company Workplace characteristics that may cause them pain.

If your score is 26-35, your Workplace Engagement level is high and you're approaching best in class. You know that complacency is not an option, so continue to do what you do well, and always be looking for opportunities to improve Workplace Engagement as your competition works to WIN your best people.

Assess: Time for a HEART™ Checkup

1. My employees can articulate their personal health and wellness needs and how my company meets them.

Strongly disagree 1 * 2 * 3 * 4 * 5 * 6 * 7 Strongly Agree

2. My employees identify and pursue their own learning needs both inside and outside the company.

Strongly disagree 1 * 2 * 3 * 4 * 5 * 6 * 7 Strongly Agree

3. My employees can articulate my company's mission and principles, and showcase how they act on them daily.

Strongly disagree 1 * 2 * 3 * 4 * 5 * 6 * 7 Strongly Agree

4. My employees are friends with each other and their team leaders outside of the office.

Strongly disagree 1 * 2 * 3 * 4 * 5 * 6 * 7 Strongly Agree

5. My employees are rewarded for taking time off and disconnecting from work.

Strongly disagree 1 * 2 * 3 * 4 * 5 * 6 * 7 Strongly Agree

Calculate your company score: Add the number of points from each answer to arrive at your total score.

If your total is 10 or less, your HEART™ Engagement level is low and your company is at a competitive disadvantage. You are likely experiencing serious engagement, retention, and recruiting challenges. There is significant danger of failure to meet sustainable profitability goals. Potential remedial steps – invest in HEART™ initiatives for your employees or they may try to find another company that will.

If your score is 11-25, your HEART™ Engagement level is average and you are likely doing something well. You may be seeing some signs that you are being disrupted by competitors with a higher score. Existing employees maybe at risk of

WIN

departure, and recruiting will likely become more difficult as candidates for roles notice company HEART™ characteristics that may cause them pain.

If your score is 26-35, your HEART™ Engagement level is high and you're approaching best in class. You know that complacency is not an option, so continue to do what you do well, and always be looking for opportunities to improve HEART™ Engagement as your competition works to WIN your best people.

Collaborate With Us

Ready to make lasting change and future-proof your workforce?

Host a WIN Company Book Club. Schedule a time for employees to come together and engage in meaningful discussion, share takeaways, and break down communication silos. You can use the discussion questions from the previous section, or email us at *WINbookauthors@gmail.com* for a list of meaningful activities.

Host a WIN Fishbowl. The "Fishbowl" method is revolutionizing how employees create meaningful discourse and share ideas, with up to 80% audience engagement. Start with 4 chairs in the front of the room, like a panel. Ask for volunteers to fill 3 of the chairs, leaving one open. Then, ask a WIN discussion question. As the 3 panelists speak, anyone from the audience can occupy the 4th seat to share their thoughts. If you'd like one of us to occupy the panel seats in-person or virtually, connect with us at *WINbookauthors@gmail.com*.

WIN

Host a WIN Thinkathon. A Thinkathon is an excellent way to address a specific culture challenge or opportunity uncovered through WIN. Like a Hackathon, a Thinkathon can last several hours to several days.

Deliver a prompt such as:
• "How can we improve our culture to accelerate employee career value and keep them relevant, influential, and in-demand?"
• "How can we improve our existing office space to engage employees at the door?"
• "How can we increase our Education in HEART™?"

Organize employees into teams, and allot them 24 hours to prepare a solution and a presentation. The winning team gets an award or, better yet, is empowered to implement their solution. If you want to learn about how we can help you organize or host a successful Thinkathon, connect with us at *WINbookauthors@gmail.com*.

Time to WIN!

Invite us to deliver an impactful keynote, panel, or workshop. The last thing you need at your next big meeting is another speaker who delivers a canned message with no lasting impact on your company culture. You need speakers who will deliver 10x their value in an engaging, interactive, and experiential format that will have your employees talking for months. If we can make such an impact on your next event, connect with us at *WINbookauthors@gmail.com*.

Help Us Continue The Research. Share with us your ideas, thoughts, and insights. Contact us at *WINbookauthors@gmail.com*.

Contact Give Value First Authors:
TLevine@AdvantageTalentInc.com
MLevine@AdvantageTalentInc.com
Contact Engaged at The Door Authors:
Michelle@Wildmor.com
Jenny@Wildmor.com
Contact Giving HEART™ Author:
chris@chrisbutsch.com

Thank you!

Acknowledgements

WIN

ACKNOWLEGEMENTS

Writing a book takes a village. Tracy, Michael, Michelle, Jenny, and Chris would like to thank our family and friends for their support. We would also like to thank the following:

Tracy Levine and Michael Levine: We would like to thank our clients and friends, many of whom are active participants among the thousands of members of the ATI Financial Executive Forum, the ATI Renaissance Executive Transition Forum, and the ATI Innovation Incubator Industry 4.0. Your first-hand experience added valuable perspective to our research for this book. Special thanks to Adrian Tatsch for book design and illustrations.

Michelle Galvani and Jenny O'Donnell: We would like to express our gratitude to some of the most innovative and employee centric companies, throughout the country, for spending time with us in preparation for this book. The insight we gained was invaluable to our research.

Acknowledgements

Chris Butsch: I would like to give special thanks to Holly Yan for polishing and perfecting passages of this book. Thanks also to Jared Kleinert for sparking invaluable connections and conversations that led to this project. And special thanks to everyone who supported my research and publication costs through Kickstarter.

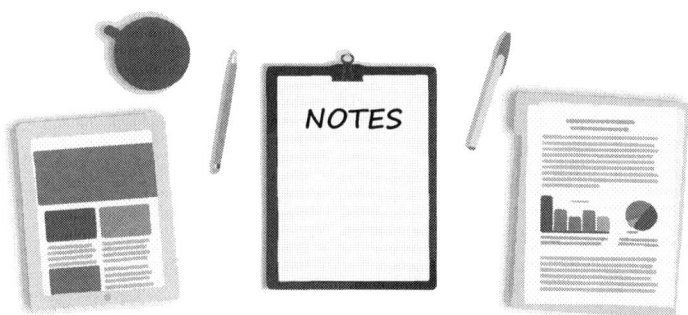

Notes

WIN

NOTES/REFERENCES

Chapter 1:
The Future of Employee Engagement is Complex

1. (7) **By 2018, the percentage of fully-engaged employees dropped to 17%.** "The Global Study of Engagement." Marcus Buckingham / ADP Research Institute. https://www.marcusbuckingham.com/research/.

Chapter 2:
Give Value First

2. (16) **Deloitte survey revealed that only 42% of organizations surveyed are made up primarily of salaried employees.** "The Workforce Ecosystem: Managing beyond the Enterprise." Deloitte Insights. https://www2.deloitte.com/us/en/insights/focus/human-capital-trends/2018/contingent-workforce-management.html.

3. (22) **LinkedIn operates the world's largest Internet-based professional network that includes more than 645 million members in over 200 countries and territories.** "About Us." LinkedIn Newsroom. https://news.linkedin.com/about-us#statistics.

4. (24) **To do that well, we need a workforce that's more representative of the users we serve.** "Diversity: Google." Google Diversity. https://diversity.google/.

Chapter 3:
Engaged At The Door

5. (47) **According to CoreNet Global, an international real estate group, the average square feet of office space per person has fallen from 225 in 2010 to 150 in 2013.** "What Shrinking Offices Mean for Your Business Center." AllWork.Space. https://allwork.space/2013/08/what-shrinking-offices-mean-for-your-business-center/#sthash.WpsOY4k5.dpuf.

6. (48) **Face-to-face interactions decreased by almost 70%, and electronic messages increased by 50%.** "New Harvard Study: Your Open-Office Plan Is Making Your Team Less Collaborative." Inc.com. https://www.inc.com/jessica-stillman/new-harvard-study-you-open-plan-office-is-making-your-team-less-collaborative.html.

7. (53) **In a recent survey, the Harvard Business Review looked into "What Employees Want Most from Their Workspaces," and here is what they found.** "What Employees Want Most from Their Workspaces." Harvard Business Review. https://hbr.org/2019/08/survey-what-employees-want-most-from-their-workspaces.

Chapter 4:
Giving HEART

8. (66) **If it was, the most lucrative industries would also have the most engaged employees (when in fact the opposite is often true – there's only a 2% overlap between pay and job satisfaction).** "Does Money Really Affect Motivation?

A Review of the Research." Harvard Business review. https://hbr.org/2013/04/does-money-really-affect-motiv.

9. (68) **All employees who spend at least some (but not all) of their time working remotely have higher engagement than those who never work remotely.** "State of the American Workplace." Gallup. https://www.gallup.com/workplace/238085/state-american-workplace-report-2017.aspx.

10. (68) **37% of employees say they would switch to a job that would allow at least part-time remote work. "50% Of The U.S. Workforce Will Soon Be Remote.** Here's How Founders Can Manage Flexible Working Styles." Forbes. https://www.forbes.com/sites/samantharadocchia/2018/07/31/50-of-the-us-workforce-will-soon-be-remote-heres-how-founders-can-manage-flexible-working-styles/#5bdac9705767.

11. (68) **Remote work improves productivity and retention by 25%.** "State of Remote Work 2017." Owl Labs. https://www.owllabs.com/state-of-remote-work/2017.

12. (69) **Sure, employees working 60% remotely can save $8000 annually in commuting costs.** "The True Cost of Commuting: You Could Buy a House Priced $15,900 More for Each Mile You Move Closer to Work." Lifehacker. https://lifehacker.com/the-true-cost-of-commuting-you-could-buy-a-house-price-5855550.

13. (69) **Health: A 2012 study in the American Journal of Preventative Medicine Linked commuting to cardiovascular disease, obesity, and lower mental health.** "Commuting Distance, Cardiorespiratory Fitness, and Metabolic Risk." American Journal of Preventative Medicine. https://www.ajpmonline.org/article/S0749-3797(12)00167-5/abstract.

14. (69) **Naturally, 82% of remote workers report lower stress and greater happiness.** "Telecommuting Reduces Stress and Increases Productivity According to a PGi Survey" PGi. http://pgi.mediaroom.com/2014-03-03-Telecommuting-Reduces-Stress-and-Increases-Productivity-According-to-PGi-Survey.

15. (69) **Education: Employees who work remotely 60-80% of the time are the most likely of all employees to strongly agree they have opportunities to learn and grow | In Gallup surveys, remote workers give their employers higher scores on "mission and purpose," indicating that "remote workers may feel more connected to their companies, despite physical distance."** "State of the American Workplace." Gallup. https://www.gallup.com/workplace/238085/state-american-workplace-report-2017.aspx.

16. (70) **Relationships: Employees who work 60-80% remotely are the most likely of all employees to strongly agree that they have a best friend at work, meaning they're more than twice as likely to stay engaged.** "Why We Need Best Friends at Work." Gallup. https://www.gallup.com/workplace/236213/why-need-best-friends-work.aspx.

17. (70) **Time: The average commute time in America is 25.4 minutes each way.** "Commute Times in Your Area: WNYC." WNYC. https://project.wnyc.org/commute-times-us/embed.html.

18.   (71) **When those other companies repealed remote work, absenteeism increased by up to 60%. "Why Are Companies Ending Remote Work?" SHRM.** https://www.shrm.org/resourcesandtools/hr-topics/employee-relations/pages/drawbacks-to-working-at-home-.aspx.

19.   (76) **Half of employees under 40 plan to quit their jobs within two years.** "Deloitte Global Millennial Survey 2019. Deloitte Insights. https://www2.deloitte.com/global/en/pages/about-deloitte/articles/millennialsurvey.html.

20.   (76) **80% of workplace gamification efforts fail to improve engagement because they try to squeeze productivity out of employees without giving HEART™.** "The Pros and Cons of a Gamified Work Culture." Fast Company. https://www.fastcompany.com/3035257/the-pros-and-cons-of-a-gamified-work-culture.

21.   (77) **Rather than gamify productivity, call center outsourcing firm LiveOps gamified training, slashing onboarding time by 80%.** "The Right (and Wrong) Way to Gamify Work." Fast Company. https://www.fastcompany.com/3063932/the-right-and-wrong-way-to-gamify-work

22. (77) **Deloitte used the same strategy to boost return traffic to Deloitte Leadership Academy by 37%.** "The Dark Side of Gamifying Work." Fast Company. https://www.fastcompany.com/90260703/the-dark-side-of-gamifying-work

23. (77) **Yes, L&D can increase engagement, but only when it gives HEART™.** "Latest Game Theory: Mixing Work and Play." The Wall Street Journal. https://www.wsj.com/articles/SB1000142405297 02042945045766615371783795248

24. (78) **62% of companies that teach creative writing, mindfulness, public speaking, and other general skills saw an immediate and measurable increase in engagement.** "How Deloitte Made Learning a Game. Harvard Business Review. https://hbr.org/2013/01/how-deloitte-made-learning-a-g

25. (78) **"When you don't act on what your people have told you are the most important issues they face, your company's culture doesn't just stay the same. It gets much, much worse."** "Your Employee Engagement Survey is Destroying Your Company Culture." Fast Company. https://www.fastcompany.com/90335847/your-engagement-survey-is-destroying-your-companys-culture

26. (79) **A 2016 Glassdoor survey found 57% of job candidates list benefits and perks as a top consideration.** "Glassdoor's 5 Job Trends to Watch in 2016." Glassdoor. https://www.glassdoor.com/blog/glassdoors-5-job-trends-watch-2016/

27. (79) **Glassdoor found that employees valued these five perks the highest because of their "life-changing potential."** "Top 20 Employee Benefits and Perks for 2017." Glassdoor. https://www.glassdoor.com/blog/top-20-employee-benefits-perks-for-2017/

28. (80) **Wellness Programs fail 90% to 95% of the time because they prioritize accountability and cost-savings over HEART™.** "The Science of Lifestyle Change." American Journal of Health Promotion. https://journals.sagepub.com/doi/10.4278/ajhp.28.1.iv

29. (80) **FitBit's coldly Orwellian sales pitch demonstrates: Business leaders recognize the burden of rising healthcare costs to their companies and their employees.** "The Case for Corporate Wellness." FitBit. https://healthsolutions.fitbit.com/corporatewellness/

Made in the USA
Columbia, SC
08 February 2020